TOOLS FOR CAREGIVERS

- **ATOS:** 0.5
- **GRL:** B
- **WORD COUNT:** 29

- **CURRICULUM CONNECTIONS:** colors

Skills to Teach

- **HIGH-FREQUENCY WORDS:** a, is, the
- **CONTENT WORDS:** bug, color, frog, grass, green, light, pepper, tractor
- **PUNCTUATION:** periods
- **WORD STUDY:** /k/, spelled c (*tractor*); long /i/, spelled *igh* (*light*); long /e/, spelled *ee* (*green*); short /u/, spelled *u* (*bug*)
- **TEXT TYPE:** information report

Before Reading Activities

- Read the title and give a simple statement of the main idea.
- Have students "walk" though the book and talk about what they see in the pictures.
- Introduce new vocabulary by having students predict the first letter and locate the word in the text.
- Discuss any unfamiliar concepts that are in the text.

After Reading Activities

Have the readers take another look at the cover of the book. Explain to them that leaves are often green. But many change color in fall and turn shades of red, orange, and yellow. Can the readers think of anything else in nature that changes color? Grass? Other plants? Animals?

Tadpole Books are published by Jump!, 5357 Penn Avenue South, Minneapolis, MN 55419, www.jumplibrary.com

Copyright ©2020 Jump. International copyright reserved in all countries. No part of this book may be reproduced in any form without written permission from the publisher.

Editor: Jenna Trnka **Designer:** Anna Peterson

Photo Credits: OmniArt/Shutterstock, cover; Tim UR/Shutterstock, 1; Efetova Anna/Shutterstock, 3 (background); Scott Hales/Dreamstime, 3 (foreground); Manuel Findeis/Shutterstock, 2tr, 4–5; smereka/Shutterstock, 2br, 6–7; Bildagentur Zoonar GmbH/Shutterstock, 2ml, 8–9; Yunhyok Choi/Shutterstock, 2tl, 10–11; yevtushenko serhii/Shutterstock, 2bl, 12–13; Lance Bellers/Dreamstime, 2mr, 14–15; imporovize/Shutterstock, 16.

Library of Congress Cataloging-in-Publication Data
Names: Peterson, Anna C., 1982– author.
Title: Green / by Anna C. Peterson.
Description: Minneapolis, MN: Jump!, Inc., (2020) | Series: Fun with colors | Includes index.
Identifiers: LCCN 2018061479 (print) | LCCN 2019001838 (ebook) | ISBN 9781641289399 (ebook) | ISBN 9781641289375 (hardcover : alk. paper) | ISBN 9781641289382 (pbk.)
Subjects: LCSH: Green—Juvenile literature. | Color—Juvenile literature.
Classification: LCC QC495.5 (ebook) | LCC QC495.5 .P477 2019 (print) | DDC 535.6—dc23
LC record available at https://lccn.loc.gov/2018061479

FUN WITH COLORS

GREEN

by Anna C. Peterson

TABLE OF CONTENTS

WORDS TO KNOW

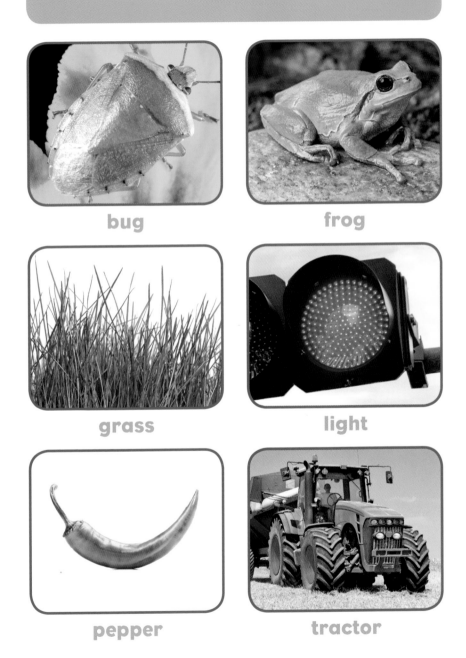

bug

frog

grass

light

pepper

tractor

GREEN

green

Green is a color.

frog

The frog is green.

tractor

The tractor is green.

The grass is green.

bug

The bug is green.

pepper ·····▶

The pepper is green.

light

The light is green.

LET'S REVIEW!

Look around you. What is green at the park?

INDEX